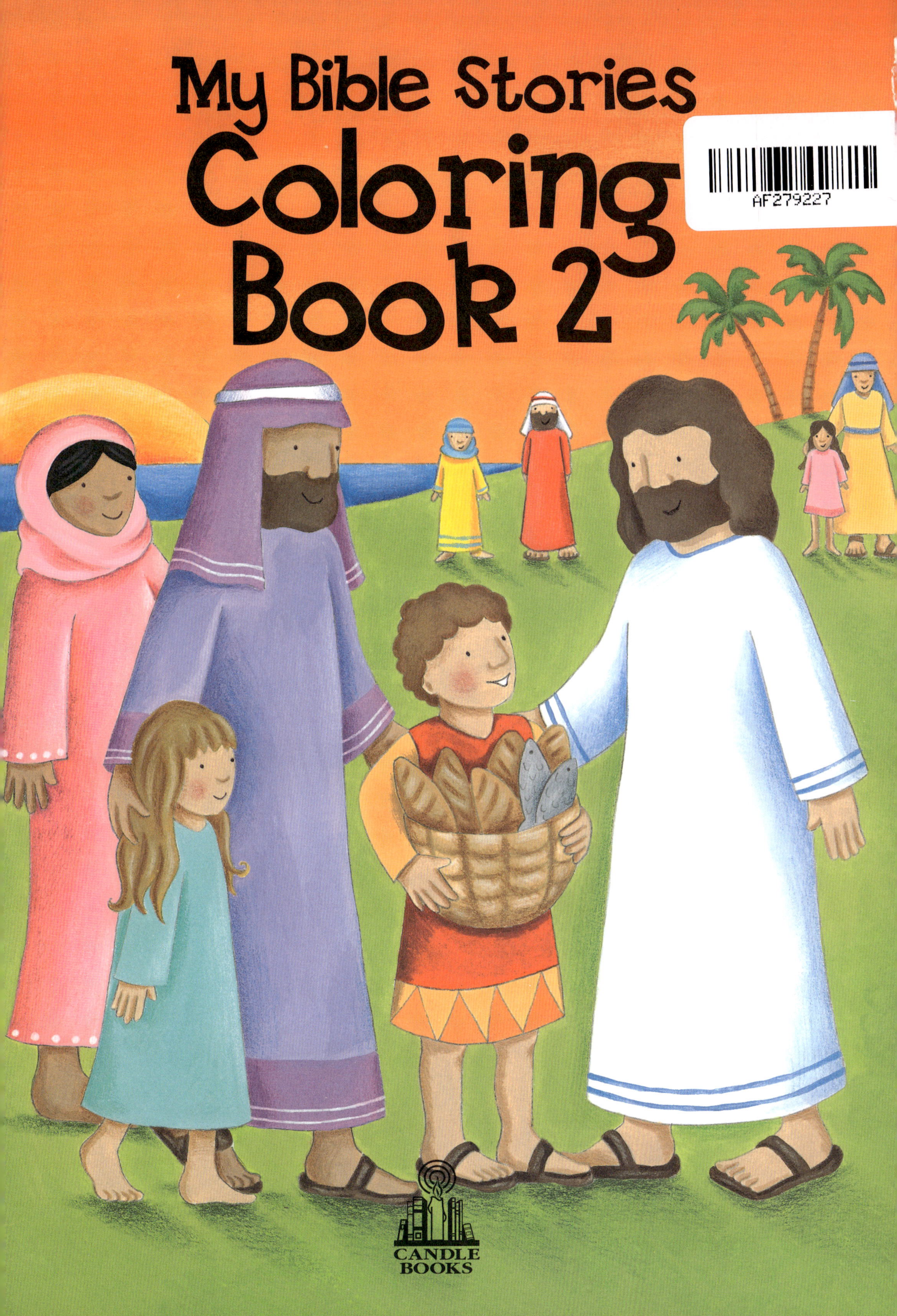

My Bible Stories
Coloring
Book 2
AF279227
CANDLE
BOOKS

Jacob has gone to sleep in the desert, with a rock for his pillow.
He is having a wonderful dream.

Jacob sees angels, climbing up and down from heaven.
You can find this story in Genesis 28:10–19.

Jacob has given his young son Joseph a wonderful coat.
But Joseph's brothers are not happy.

"Why does Joseph get all the best things from our father?" they complain.
You can find this story in Genesis 37:2–11.

Little David is just a shepherd boy.
Goliath is a fierce giant.

But only David is brave enough to fight the huge soldier.
God helps him to beat Goliath.
You can find this story in 1 Samuel 17:20–50.

Jonah was sailing in this boat when a huge storm arose.
The sailors throw him into the waves.
Jonah is afraid he will drown.

But God has sent a great fish to swallow him.
After three days, the fish spits Jonah out on to the seashore.
You can find this story in Jonah chapter 1.

John was baptizing people in the river.
Jesus said to John, "Please baptize me, too!"

As Jesus came out of the water, God said,
"This is my son! I'm so very pleased with him."
You can find this story in Matthew 3:13–17.

This boy left his home and family.
But now he has decided to come back.
His father runs to welcome him.

How pleased he is to see his lost son.
God is happy too, when he welcomes people who are lost.
You can find this story in Luke 15:11–32.

Jesus has been telling stories to a huge crowd of people.
Now they are very hungry. This little boy has brought his lunch
to Jesus: five loaves and two fish.

Jesus shares the food with the whole crowd.
There's more than enough for everyone!
You can find this story in John 6:5–13.

When Jesus comes to town, everyone wants to see him.
Zacchaeus is very short. So he climbs a tree to get a good view.
"Come down, Zacchaeus," says Jesus. "I want to visit your home."
You can find this story in Luke 19:1–10.